A Character Building Book ™

Learning About Dedication from the Life of
Frederick Douglass

Sam Marlowe

The Rosen Publishing Group's
PowerKids Press ™
New York

Published in 1996 by The Rosen Publishing Group, Inc.
29 East 21st Street, New York, NY 10010

First Edition

Book design: Erin McKenna

Photo credits: Cover © Archive Photos; pp. 4, 11, 15, 16, 19 © Corbis-Bettmann; pp. 7, 8, 12, 20 © The Bettmann Archive.

Marlowe, Sam.
Learning dedication from the life of Frederick Douglass / Sam Marlowe.
        p.   cm. — (A character building book)
    Includes index.
    Summary: A simple biography of a man who dedicated his life to fighting for equal rights for African Americans.
    ISBN 0-8239-2425-4
    1. Douglass, Frederick, 1817?–1895—Juvenile literature. 2. Abolitionists—United States—Biography—Juvenile literature. 3. Afro-American abolitionists—Biography—Juvenile literature. 4. Slaves—United States—Biography—Juvenile literature. [1. Douglass, Frederick, 1817?–1895. 2. Abolitionists. 3. Afro-Americans—Biography.] I. Title. II. Series.
E449.D75M36 1996
973.8'092—dc20
[B]   96-6996
                                                                                              CIP
                                                                                              AC

Manufactured in the United States of America

Table of Contents

Fighting Slavery

Frederick Douglass was born Frederick Bailey, a slave in the United States, in 1817. To be a slave meant that you belonged to someone else. You worked from morning till night for no pay. You lived wherever your **master** (MAS-ter), the person who owned you, decided. And you had to do whatever he or she wanted. As a slave, Frederick had no freedom.

Frederick, like all slaves, knew that slavery was wrong. He **dedicated** (DED-ih-kay-tid) his life to fighting the system of slavery.

◀ *Frederick, like many African Americans, dedicated his life to fighting slavery.*

Slavery in the Americas

When Frederick was born, slavery had been in North and South America for more than 200 years. European slave traders had made a business of capturing and buying people from Africa. Those slaves were then sold to people in North America, South America, and the Caribbean. On the trip across the ocean, slaves were treated like animals. They were given little food or water. Many died of hunger or disease. Many who did survive were sold to wealthy landowners in the southern United States.

Slaves were often sold at public markets as if they were animals. ▶

Growing Up as a Slave

When he was 6 years old, Frederick was taken from his mother's shack to work in the master's house. He had to work very hard. He was often beaten. Frederick and the other slave children in the house were fed only scraps of food. They wore rough cotton shirts. They were often hungry and cold in the winter. Frederick was unhappy, but he was also very smart. He worked hard. He knew that he would one day fight for a better life for himself and other slaves.

◄ *Many Americans did not agree with slavery or the way slave owners treated their slaves.*

Learning to Read

When he was 10, Frederick was sold to another master in Baltimore, Maryland. The new master's wife was kind. She taught Frederick to read. But that was against the law. People were afraid that if slaves knew how to read, they would learn about freedom. Then they would try to **escape** (es-KAYP). When the master learned what his wife was doing, he was very angry. He did not allow his wife to continue teaching Frederick. But Frederick did not give up. He **devoted** (dee-VOH-ted) himself to continuing his education.

Frederick took his education seriously. He knew that it would one day help free him. ▶

Antislavery Movement

Frederick secretly continued to read. He learned about people who wanted to end slavery. He heard of people who helped free slaves. He learned that many Americans agreed that slavery was wrong. He found out that some slaves had been set free by their masters. Other slaves were able to buy their freedom from their masters. Frederick started thinking about how he could become free too. He knew that if he could get to one of the Northern states, he would be free. But it would be a very dangerous journey.

◀ *Studying gave Frederick ideas and helped him become a free man.*

Standing Up for Himself

When Frederick was a teenager, his master sold him to another master who owned a **plantation** (plan-TAY-shun). Even though he worked hard and well, Frederick was often beaten. One day, Frederick had had enough. When the master tried to beat him, Frederick stood up for himself. He fought back. The master never beat him again.

The plantations of the South were home to many slaves. ▶

Escape from Slavery

Freedom was always on Frederick's mind. Once, he and a few other slaves planned to escape. But someone told the master their plan. Frederick was caught and thrown in jail.

Later, Frederick was sent back to Baltimore to work as a slave in a shipyard. He met many free African Americans. He met Anna Murray, who later became his wife. With the help of Anna and others, Frederick escaped. He went to New York City, where slavery was not allowed. He changed his name to Frederick Douglass to avoid slave catchers. But Frederick was free. His dedication had paid off.

◀ *Once free, Frederick dedicated his life to helping others become free.*

Speaking Out

As soon as he was free, Frederick began working to end slavery. He traveled to many cities in the U.S., England, and Ireland giving speeches about the horrors of slavery. Slaves had no **legal** (LEE-gul) rights. They were not allowed to own anything of value. It was legal for masters to beat, whip, or even kill their slaves. Frederick started an antislavery newspaper. He wrote powerful articles that said slavery should be stopped. He wrote a book about his life. He convinced many people that slavery should not be legal.

Frederick began an antislavery newspaper to tell people how horrible slavery was. ▶

HON. FREDERICK DOUGLASS

EX-SENATOR BRUCE

EX-SENATOR REVELS

The End of Slavery

The Southern states wanted to keep slavery. They were willing to separate from the Northern states to do it. The Northern states believed that slavery should not be legal. And they were willing to fight to keep the country together. For that reason, in 1861, the Civil War began. The Union Army of the North fought the Confederate Army of the South. Frederick helped set up the first African American unit in the Union Army. The Civil War lasted 4 years. The North won the war. Slavery was out-lawed. And the North and South remained one country, the United States of America.

◀ *All of Frederick's efforts paid off. Slavery was finally outlawed.*

Dedication Until the End

Although slavery had ended, African Americans were not treated as **equals** (EE-kwulz) by many Americans. Frederick dedicated his life to fighting for equal rights for African Americans. He wrote and spoke out against **violence** (VY-o-lents) toward African Americans. Frederick Douglass dreamed of all Americans living together in peace. He dedicated his life to this dream, and he never gave up. Frederick Douglass died more than 100 years ago. He is remembered as a national hero.

Glossary

dedicate (DED-ih-kayt) Work hard for a cause.

devote (dee-VOH-ted) Dedicate time to something.

equal (EE-kwul) Someone having the same rights as someone else.

escape (es-KAYP) To leave a place that you're not supposed to leave.

legal (LEE-gul) Allowed by the law.

master (MAS-ter) Person who legally owns someone else.

plantation (plan-TAY-shun) Large piece of land on which a family and workers lived and grew crops, such as cotton.

violence (VY-o-lents) Hurting someone or something.

Index

A
abuse, 9, 14, 18
antislavery
movement, 13,
18
antiviolence, 22

C
childhood, slave,
9
Civil War, 21

E
education, 10
equality, 22
escape, 10, 17

F
freedom, 13, 17,
18

J
jail, 17

M
master, 5, 9, 10,
13, 14, 17

N
newspaper,
antislavery, 18

P
plantation, 14

R
read, learning to,
10, 13

S
slavery, 5, 6, 9,
13, 17, 18,
21, 22
slave traders, 6

U
Union Army, first
African
American unit,
21

24